Lost Cities

Contents

Written by Murray Pile

Introduction

Many civilizations have left unexplained traces. Stonehenge in England, pyramids in both Egypt and Mexico, and the city of Petra in Jordon are all still surrounded by mystery.

Stories told about lost cities are always full of adventure and danger. Some of these stories were passed down by word of mouth, and others were recorded in ancient writings. Some of these places have been found, and others are still lost.

Pompeii was buried when Mt Vesuvius erupted in AD 79.

Two examples of famous cities that were lost, then found, are Machu Picchu and Pompeii. Machu Picchu is in Peru, South America and Pompeii is in Italy, which is in Europe.

Machu Picchu was founded by the Incas in South America.

Machu Picchu

Machu Picchu is an old Inca city that was rediscovered in 1911 by American explorer Hiram Bingham. But the local farmers had always known about the ancient city.

The Incas were South American Indian people who ruled a large empire that stretched along the west coast of South America. This empire was conquered by Spanish invaders in the sixteenth century.

Hiram Bingham believed that Machu Picchu might have been the last stronghold of the Incas who were fleeing from the capital of their empire, Cuzco, Peru, after the Spanish invaders arrived.

Where Is Machu Picchu?

Machu Picchu is in the Andes Mountains in Peru, South America. It is about 50 miles (80 km) northwest of Cuzco.

Machu Picchu is on a ridge 7,000 feet (2,134 m) above sea level, between two mountain peaks, high above the Urubamba River. The ruined city covers about five square miles (13 km^2).

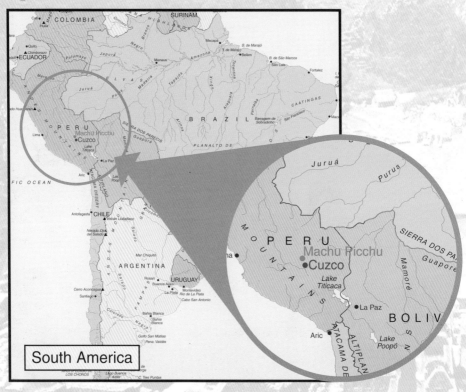

South America

What Does Machu Picchu Look Like?

When the lost city of Machu Picchu was discovered, it was choked with heavy jungle growth. The growth was cleared to show a terraced city of well-engineered buildings, connected by hundreds of stairways and walkways. The walkways led to plazas, homes, and a cemetery.

Machu Picchu is a terraced city.

Most of the buildings that were found in 1911 were one-room stone houses arranged around internal courts. These buildings are made of a stone called granite. The large pieces of stone were carefully cut to fit tightly together.

How Did People Live In Machu Picchu?

People are not sure about the history of Machu Picchu. Some people think that Machu Picchu was a place where the royal family went when they were not staying in Cuzco. Some buildings appear to be houses for farmers and servants of the royal family.

Other people think that Machu Picchu was a religious retreat because there are many shrines.

Flat terraces in and around Machu Picchu were probably used to grow crops.

There are many terraces on the slopes of Machu Picchu.

History

People who study history think that the people who lived in Machu Picchu left the city sometime in the middle of the 17th century. It was at that time that the Spanish invaded the Inca Empire searching for gold and other treasures to take home to Spain. It is thought that some of the Inca people retreated into the hills around Machu Picchu.

The History of Machu Picchu

16th Century	17th Century	18th Century
Machu Picchu built	Spanish invasion of Inca Empire	

At the time the Spanish did not know that Machu Picchu existed. Today, the lost city of Machu Picchu is a famous tourist attraction. Many people travel to Machu Picchu each year to see the ruins of this ancient lost city. Recently, other lost cities have been found in the area around Machu Picchu.

19th Century	20th Century	21st Century
	Rediscovery of Machu Picchu Some tourists visit Machu Picchu	Machu Picchu becomes a popular tourist attraction

Machu Picchu and the Inca Trail 14-day Hotel and Camping Trip

Come with us on the most famous hike in the Andes. Our trek follows the secret Inca Trail from Cuzco through the mountains and jungle to the lost city of Machu Picchu.

We hike to an altitude of 7,875 feet (2,400 m).

This is the best possible way for you to visit this magnificent lost city. We spend two days exploring the area around Cuzco and getting used to the thin mountain air.

Group Size

Minimum 8, maximum 16, plus the group leader and local guides and porters.

Accommodation

You will stay in hotels and also spend some nights camping along the Inca Trail.

Itinerary

Day 1
Meet in Lima.

Day 2
Fly from Lima to Cuzco.

Day 3
Explore the ruins above Cuzco.

Day 4
Start hike.

Day 10
Arrive Machu Picchu.

Day 11
Explore Machu Picchu.

Day 12
Take train to the Sacred Valley.
Explore the Sacred Valley.
Return to Cuzco.

Day 14
Return to Lima, where tour ends.

Food

In Cuzco we provide only breakfast.

We provide all the food while we are hiking.

Clothing

In addition to your usual clothes, please make sure that you have well-fitting boots. You will also need to bring with you a warm waterproof jacket.

Dates and Prices

Trips run May to September

Start	Finish
May 27	June 9
June 22	July 5
July 22	August 4
August 19	September 1
September 16	September 29

Please check our website www.machuexplore.com for current prices.

You will need an up-to-date passport and a visa.

This is a C level hike. Please read the C level information to see if this trip is right for you.

C level – strenuous hiking.

If you undertake this trip you will need to be very fit. We walk each day with back packs for between six and eight hours. Most of our walking will be in the mountains. It will be remote and there could be big changes in the weather between day and night.

If you have been hiking before, you will be able to manage this trip. If you have not been hiking before, you should prepare yourself for this trip by walking in steep places with a pack on your back.

Pompeii

Pompeii is one of the most famous lost cities in the world. Pompeii vanished suddenly on August 24 of the year AD 79 when the volcano Vesuvius erupted.

The volcano, which is less than six miles (10 km) northwest of Pompeii, had been quiet for more than 1,200 years. When Vesuvius erupted, Pompeii was buried under volcanic ash and cinders to a depth of 15–30 feet (4.6–9 m). For more than 15 centuries, the ruins stayed buried.

Where Was Pompeii?

Pompeii is an ancient city of Italy in the Campania region. It was built at the mouth of the Samus River, now called the Sarno River.

What Did Pompeii Look Like?

Pompeii was a city of more than 10,000 people. Like any city, it had many buildings, paved streets, hundreds of houses, a large arena, and a port.

Two famous places in Pompeii, which can be identified today through the ruins, are the Forum, and the Temple of Jupiter.

More than 2,000 people were killed when Pompeii was buried.

The Forum was the busiest part of any Roman town. This was the place where there were government buildings, temples, and the market. There usually was a large open square with many statues. On the north side of the Pompeii Forum was the Temple of Jupiter.

The Temple of Jupiter was already ancient at the time of the Vesuvius eruption. It was a grand building in which the people of Pompeii worshipped Jupiter, who they believed was the ruler of the universe.

The Basilica was also an important building in Pompeii. Its high interior was divided by columns into a wide hall and two side aisles. This building served as a courtroom and a market, and it was also where all the banking and trading activities took place.

How Did People Live In Pompeii?

Pompeii was a bustling Roman city with wealthy landowners, merchants, bankers, and store owners. The store owners usually made the items that they sold in the front of their shops. People walking past would stop to chat, or barter for the goods for sale.

Life in a City

People bank money

Shop at stores

Worship in temples

Go to races

Go to school

The activities in Pompeii were much like the activities in a modern city.

People worshipped in temples, went to plays, watched races and fights, and relaxed in public pools called baths. Boys went to school and learned to read, write, and count.

Pompeii	Modern City
✔	✔
✔	✔
✔	✔
✔	✔
✔	✔

What Caused Pompeii To Become Lost?

When Mount Vesuvius erupted, it covered the city in ash and cinders. Many people were able to escape, but it is believed that nearly 2,000 people died. Some were crushed by falling roofs or columns, while others were suffocated by the hot gases and ash. Many drowned in rough seas.

The city was so thoroughly covered in volcanic matter that the survivors moved on and rebuilt elsewhere. Eventually, Pompeii was forgotten.

Explore the Ruins of Pompeii

Spend five days reliving the past. The tour departs from Rome on Thursdays.

This amazing tour takes you back through time to the days when Pompeii was a busy, wealthy city, before it was destroyed by the eruption of Mount Vesuvius.

See what the architect, Domenico Fontana first uncovered in the late 1500s when he was digging a channel to take water to a nearby town.

You can still walk down the cobbled streets of Pompeii

Itinerary

Day 1
Meet in Rome. You will go from here by bus to Pompeii.

Day 2
Walk down cobblestone streets and look into houses where the people of Pompeii lived. Our guides will take you back in time so that you will be able to imagine how the people lived.

Day 3
You visit the Forum. This was the busiest place in any Roman town. Our guides will explain the buildings and what went on in each one of them.

Day 4
Today you visit temples and the Arena. You will be able to feel the grandeur of the temples and the excitement of the chariot races.

Day 5
Today completes your journey into the past, and we return to Rome, where the tour ends.

What's included
Experienced guides
All food and accommodation
Bus trip to and from Rome

Glossary

arena – A place where gladiators fought.

cemetery – A place where people are buried.

granite – A very hard rock.

Jupiter – The main god of the Romans.

market – A place where people sell and buy things.

plaza – A public square in a city or town.

temple(s) – A building where people worship their god(s).

terraces – Flat areas that rise above each other like stairs, but higher and longer.